MW00883126

for My Beautiful Black Sister

NATHAN B. BROOKEN

PAGE PUBLISHING, INC.
New York, NY

First originally published by Page Publishing, Inc. 2015

Cover Design by
Faith Howard

Lips Provided by
Faith, Alexis, and Tiffany Howard

ISBN 978-1-68213-243-2 (pbk)
ISBN 978-1-68213-244-9 (digital)

Printed in the United States of America

The author would appreciate you
filling out the survey at the end of this
work and returning it to him.

Forward your remarks to
nathanbbrooken@yahoo.com.

Thanks a million.

Acknowledgments

I'll always be grateful to the following people whom without their love, guidance, and support, I wouldn't have completed this project: My family, especially my sister Faith, who edited, critiqued, and typed every poem in this volume and the next two. The late George and Martha Washington, whom I miss tremendously. The late Deacon Clawrence Jones, Hubert Watson, Altamese Watson, Bill and Barbara Pope, Dr. Jeff Butler, Dr. Edgar Wycoff, Dr. Otis Holloway-Owens, David and Stephanie Murphy, Chris and Tammy McDeaough, Joyce Council, Daisy Johnson, Barbara Marbury, Raymond King, Chris Sineath, Reba Johnson, Jan Freeman, Jane Green, lifelong friend Ronald Barnard, Jean Marie Thibodeau, the late Maria Pate, Gail Marston, Charlotte Reeves, the late Imogene Walker, Marcia Hurst, Mona Hurst, Norma Beasley, Savannah Sirmons, the staff at Englewood High School, especially Alfreda Fitzpatrick, Brenda Harris, Carol Wurzbach, and Rebecca Cray.

Introduction

Mother, these are for you and black
women all over the world.

Dear Sweetheart

Dear Sweetheart
I love you
So much
I think about
You all the
Time
You are
My strength
The song in
My heart
The thought
On my mind
Joy is all
You've
Ever given
Me and for
This reason
I say thanks
Much love.
Success
Respect

CHAPTER 1

For Those in Need of a Lift

CHAPTER 1

For Those in Need of a Lift

I find it appalling that most of today's literature attempting to explain where black women have come from and are headed center primarily around sex and relationships as if they are the only entities any group of women concern themselves with. What about our women's future? Are there things they can do to curtail the downward spiral of our children and communities? Has every black woman been in a bad relationship? Are all black men dogs? Are we the only people who have abandoned our responsibilities for pleasure?

What one experiences stems from their choices and not the color of their skin. Irregardless of what we think of a situation, we must remember it is our opinion. Besides, some people prefer to be alone, and all of them aren't women or black. Here I am merely wishing any black woman who has ever suffered any kind of setback a full and speedy recovery.

I Am a Black Woman

My life
Is a
Constant
Challenge,
To
Sustain
Myself
Experience
True love,
Avoid
Heartache,
Convince
Myself
It's up
To
Me
To carry
On,
I am a
Black woman

A Black Woman at Work

I've come
A long way,
Yet
Still I grumble,
The pay is
Good,
Conditions
Okay,
But what I
Don't see is
Troubling,
Will likely never
Change
My Fathers,
Sons,
Daughters,
Could perform
Many of these
Tasks,
But aren't given
The chance,
Color line
Gone my ass,

This room
Is full
Of
Many not as
Talented as
Myself
Some I've
Trained,
Who like others
Will ascend
Much Quicker than
I,
Lord,
Where are you
When my people
Need you so
Much?
Amen

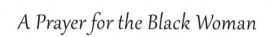

A Prayer for the Black Woman

Lord be with
The black woman
For great are
Her chances
Of being
Alone,
Pour your
Grace upon
Her,
So that she
Might remember
You're still in
Control,
Haven't forsaken
Her,
And though probably
Not convinced,
Happiness
Is attainable,
To trust and obey,
Not grieve or surrender,
Remember
Her
Unyielding
Devotion
Amen

Love without Sex

Love without sex
Would do the
Black woman
Much Good
For the other
Tenants of love
She seldom feels
Sure sex is
Great
But it can't
Greet one at
The door,
Tuck them in
At night,
Call to see
If everything is
Okay
Spring a surprise
Upon them
As they
Come home from
Work,
Help with the chores
Protect one from
The evils of this
Society

A glass of
Wine,
Being out on
A date,
Cruising in
A car
Like a kiss
Are easy
To attain,
Black man love
Your woman
Unconditionally

For the Sexually Abused

Look up
At
The clouds,
And let
Them
Remind you
How far
You can soar,
Few things here
Are of any
Solace
For something
Stolen,
Don't be afraid
To cry,
God's Arms are
Open,
His angels
Weeping,
Hoping you
Remember
How much you're
Needed

I Watched Her

I watched her,
Although confined
To a bed,
I wondered who
Had whom,
Did the disease
Have her or
Did she have the
Disease (Aids),
For the message
She conveyed
I've heard from
So many black women
Young and old,
And wonder does
This song spurt from
Their souls
I'm not bitter,
With what
I've been through,
This won't get
The best of me
Either,
I'm wise,
I'm strong,
Weeping is
How I laugh

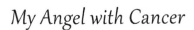

My Angel with Cancer

My angel with
Cancer,
Laugh a little,
Recall the joy
You are,
Bring,
Will always be,
The difference
You've made
Is too important
To be forgotten,
The doors you
Opened
Many more will
Pass through,
Laugh a little,
A frown
Like many others
Don't deserve
You,
Won't accomplish
Half the things
Your living
Has

Who Once Abused Drugs

Look at her,
All wobbly,
Quite confused
However when she
Abandons
Her desire
For this
Tool of the devil,
No physical
Or
Visible marks
Will exist unless
She confesses
Her mistakes,
No one will ever
Know
My sister,
Queen,
Who once
Abused drugs,
Smile
My love,
You're in
My prayers

Still You Are a Queen

Young
Black mother,
Be not ashamed
Of your child,
Still you are
A queen,
The fool who
Abandoned you only
Violated your honor,
He didn't
Corrupt your soul
Still you are
A queen,
Despite this dilemma,
Like so many
Before you,
You'll contribute mightily
To the world

A Wish

Lord,
One of your
Angels
Has had her
Wings
Clipped,
The despair
Of
Going unloved,
Appreciated
Caused her to
Collapse,

Satan
Is beside himself,
The
Thought of a
Thousand souls in
Hell
Delights him,
Help the incarcerated
Black woman
Gather her feathers

Heaven
Needs her,
I need her,
But
Mostly our people,
The love she
Is
Capacity in which
She can serve,
Few
Can afford not
To experience,
Show her the
Difference
You assigned her
To make,
That what she
Didn't receive from
Others,
Lies within herself
Amen

Fists

Fists have launched
Wars,
Ripped apart
Foundations,
Shattered glass,
Hewn wood,
Many of humanity's
Greatest atrocities
They've labored in
When swinging,
Mostly at others
Or
To inflict harm
I'm sure if
Fists could speak,
They'd boast
About their many
Misdeeds,
But there's one
They'll never be
Able to say
I destroyed,
The black woman

Sister Don't Cry

Dry your eyes
Sweetheart
Don't cry,
You have much
To be proud
Of,
In your right
Hand is more
Strength
Than most people
Acquire,
And Jesus in
All his glory
When he wept,
Dried his tears
With your hair,
And when he
Arose,
You was the
First
To greet him,
Sister don't
Cry

On the Bottom

You're not a
Whore,
Neither are you
A bitch,
For nothing is
Barbaric about your
Demeanor,
Then again how
Could it,
When so many
Women wish they
Had your
Hair,
Looks,
Figure,

Envy your
Eyes,
Lips,
Voice,
So smile
Black woman
Don't be down,
The next time
Someone refers to
You
In such
Derogatory terms
Leave them
Where they're
Most likely to
Remain
On the bottom

Sure Doesn't

Unfortunate as it
Is
Sometimes your
Best
Goes unnoticed,
Means nothing
To those
Whom you love,
But
I'm not worried
I know you,
The next step
If you don't
Figure out,
You'll create
Then once again
A smile
Will be wondering
Is death
The only thing
That knocks
Black women
Down?
Cause divorce
Sure doesn't.

Bloom, Black Flower, Bloom

Black flower
Oh how you
Bloom,
Be not afraid
For the Lord
Is with thee,
Stand firm my
Love,
And trouble will
Flee
The path you
Tread need not
Be filled with
Sorrow,
Trust in God,
Listen to
Your heart,
Develop your
Mind,
There's no
Reward in
Fear,

Compromise is
For the foolish,
Happiness flourishes
Only amongst the
Wise,
So Bloom
Black flower
Bloom,
Bloom my
Love,
Reach for the
Sky

My Daughter

My daughter is
Gonna know
For I'm gonna
Tell her,
First and foremost,
You belong to yourself,
Seek the best
Sweetheart
You deserve it,
That's not my opinion
It's God's
Reward no one
Who hasn't respected
You,
Put forth their best
Effort to make
You smile,
There's no harm in
Saying no,
And don't ever get in
The habit of saying
Yes

It's a fool's favorite response
Wherever you travel,
Take love with you
Don't ever settle,
Demand!
For in this world,
There's two kinds of
People
Those who step
And those who are
Stepped upon

CHAPTER 2

In Memory

CHAPTER 2

In Memory

I don't have any children, but still I find myself wondering what kind of impact I will have on them. Will I be a great father, the kind of leader that will make heaven proud?

Besides providing them with the essentials, I hope to be a living example of right from wrong, the virtue of patience and respect, and the joy of an honest day's work. I firmly believe that many of today's problems are due to a lack of these qualities in our homes, schools, and even our churches.

As a child and for much of my adult life, I wasn't the most expressive person in the world. I kept a lot of my emotions bottled up inside. Some, I've only recently come to grips with, and it was through poetry and song, not open dialog. This is my way of saying thanks to God and to the many black women who graced my life, presence, and soul. What they were to me, I hope I've been to someone. For if I

do, I know it'll make their burdens a little lighter. I believe many will agree with this; there are some in their graves making a greater contribution to life than some living.

- A Black Woman
- To Be Happy
- I Know Thoughts
- Everywhere I Go
- The One
- God Gave Me an Angel
- Half the Job
- Convinced
- Especially Beautiful
- Undivided Attention

A Black Woman

A black woman
First loved me,
A black woman
Lifted my soul
From the depths
Of despair,
A black woman
Awakened my
Desire,
Sparked my
Confidence,
It is a
Black woman
I want to
Marry,
A black woman
I want to
Be buried next
To

To Be Happy

To be
Happy,
I need not
Live my life
Over,
Just some
Of
The moments
We
Shared

I Know Thoughts

I know thoughts
I'll never
Forget,
Mighty thoughts
When once on
My mind,
I rejoice
Seek to if
Not be near
At least hear,
Beautiful thoughts
I'm sure
If we're allowed
To
Grace the life
Of another,
Their world would
Sparkle
They'd realize
God exists,
Exceeds
Everything
Written and Spoken
About him

Everywhere I Go

Everywhere I go
I'm going to
Take you with
Me,
For what the
Mere thought of
You
Provides me with
Will make my
Journey
Prosperous,
My worries few,
Myself a
Conqueror

The One

One night as
I was about
To lie down,
I thought about
The one
My soul admires,
And the bitterness
Of
A rejection
Leapt from my
Countenance
Like a frog,
I laughed out
Loud
Tickled one so
Far away
Could still lift
My spirits

God Gave Me an Angel

God gave me
An angel
Yes he did,
She used to
Teach me as
She sat rocking
In her chair
I on her
Step
The joy of
Love and work,
Never give up,
My son,
Press forward
Knock on as
Many doors
As you can
God gave me
An angel,
Sweeter than
One need be,
Who went without
Undergarments

So
I could eat
The insults of
Others she tossed
Aside
Caused darkness,
Even ole man winter
To tremble
The rain wait
Until she had found
Herself a seat on
The bus
Trust in the
Lord,
Any situation
You come out
Alive
Is a good one,
God gave me
An angel,
Who taught me
To smile
Anything that doesn't
Enlighten you isn't
Knowledge,
She encouraged me
Read, read, then read
Some more

Exercise
Your mind as well
As your body
Ask, listen, speak
Only when appropriate
Don't argue,
It's a waste
Of time
Here,
I'd like you
To have this.
God gave me
An angel,
Why is this lady
Always looking over
My shoulder?
She wasn't being
Mean
Just making sure
I did a
Good job
Nathan,
Anything less than
Your best
Is a waste of
Time

I realized at
A young age,
God gave me
An angel
Since I can't
Do more,
I'll say a
Prayer
For you,
You deserve something
Nice
You've done well,
This one was
Really special
Thank you Jesus
I know your
Love never wanes
And many times
When we've given
Up,
You've just begun
God gave me
An angel

Half the Job

When I have
Kids,
I want them
To be
Well behaved,
Possessors of
A good heart,
Sound mind
Respect their
Elders,
Love God,
All Mankind
They
Will
If I do
Half the job
My mother
Did raising
Me

Especially Beautiful

Many times when
I look up
Into the sky,
And see
A beautiful star,
I wonder if
It's you,
Smiling down on
Me
For the joy
You brought me
Doesn't exist
Anymore,
The bloom of
Flowers aren't
Pretty enough,
The whisk of
The wind too thin,
My imagination
Incapable of
Conceiving,
I
Know it's you
Mother
Cause many times
When I'm down,
The stars look
Especially Beautiful

Undivided Attention

I don't have
A throne,
But I know
How it feels
To be a
King,
I don't have
A vault,
But I've felt
The joys of
Being rich,
I don't have
A garden,
But I've come
Upon many
Flowers,
How you ask?
Through your
Undivided
Attention

CHAPTER 3

Sheroes

CHAPTER 3

Sheroes

An extension of chapter 2, the goal here was the element of surprise. As with my mother and some of her friends, I firmly believe that God allowed each of these fine women to enter my life and at the right time. Their presence contributed greatly to what Mrs. Simmons spent countless hours trying to get me to see.

- A Black Mother
- Mrs. Simmons
- What a Sweet Love
- Mrs. Jackson
- Mimic
- How You Doing?
- Mary
- Mrs. Mildred K. White
- Mrs. Durham's Room
- I Love You Too, Miss Robinson
- The Same Way
- So Special
- Julie's Concern
- Jacqueline
- Rosita

A Black Mother

If
I had to be
Someone besides
Myself,
I would have
Been
A
Black mother

For regardless
Of
What obstacles
I faced,
I would've overcome
Them,
Laughed more,
Never been

Nearly trampled
By poverty,
I'd known
I was loved
Appreciated myself,
So
That when I
Died,
I would've gone
To heaven

Mrs. Simmons

Wasn't long ago
I was looking
At my transcripts
From school,
The progress
I made amazed
Me,
However,
The joy I
Felt,
I owe to
You,
For your love
Was the catalyst
That not only
Improved
My grades,
But
My life
As well

What a Sweet Love

What a sweet love
You are,
When I arise
After greeting me,
You wish me
A great day
When I come in,
You greet me
With a smile,
Then remind me
While away,
I was on
Your mind
What a sweet love
When you're not
Asking me
If there's something
I need,

You're asking if
There's something
I can do,
Last night
I put you in
My prayers
'Cause I know
I'm in yours,
Thanks
Miss Pearl
What a sweet love
You are
The kind I hope
To find

Mrs. Jackson

Me and
Mrs. Jackson
Talk all the
Time,
To her it
Is
Conversation,
But to me
Comfort for
A tortured
Soul

Mimic

How Maxine
Is able
To smile
In the
Midst of
All this
Turmoil,
Is something
I admire,
Hope to
Someday
Mimic

How You Doing?

Mrs. Johnson
Is more than
My Sunday School
Teacher
She is my
Friend,
Inspiration
One that if
Success
Shall ever find
Me,
I hope feels
Proud
For since
My mother
Departed,
Not a time
Has passed
Wherein she didn't
Ask me
How you doing?

Mary

Mary helped Preserve
The country,
But seldom is
She mentioned
Her alertness
Made
Grant's and Sherman's
Job much easier
She worked at
Risk
So that others
Might have
What
Few care about
Anymore
Freedom

Mrs. Mildred K. White

When I first
Met you,
I knew you
Were
Special
The joy you
Provided me with
I not only
Wrapped around
My heart,
But took to
Class, home, and
Away to college
Many times
During my
Darkest moments,
Toughest decisions,
I would reflect
On what we
Shared
Then feel better,
Not
Because you loved
Me
But for letting
Me
Love you back

Mrs. Durham's Room

Mrs. Durham's
Room
Is a great
Place to be,
For it is
Full
Of
What
The
World
Could use
A lot
More
Of
Love

I Love You Too, Miss Robinson

This lady is
Always
Fussing
At me,
But I don't
Mind
For if
I should
Amount to
Something,
She like
So
Many of the
Wonderful
Black women
Who have
Graced
My life,
Will be grinning
From
Ear to ear
Saying
That's my
Boy,
I love you too
Miss Robinson

The Same Way

I love to
Hear
Miss Cleo
Talk about
Mama,
It's good
To know
One so sweet
Was thought
Of
By another
The same way

So Special

Mother once told
Me
That in life,
There would be
Those you'd never
Forget
At that time,
I thought
I had already
Met
Them all,
But I hadn't
And it's
With great honor
I add
Mrs. Fuller
To my list
What I feel
For her in
My heart,
I'm not going
To attempt to
Describe,
But it's oh
So
Special

Julie's Concern

Julie's concern
Keeps me
Going,
When I feel
Like
Giving up,
I think about
How much
She
Wants me to
Succeed,
Then start over
If ever I
Escape
The hell
I now endure,
I'll reflect
Back on
Julie's concern

Jacqueline

She eases
My burdens,
Reminds me
To hold
My
Head high
They say
When times are
At their
Worst,
God is at
His best,
I know this
To be true,
For when talking
With Jacqueline,
I feel his
Presence

Rosita

Is there one
Sweeter
Than Rosita
Such a
Joy to have
On my mind
In my heart
One day
I'm gonna write
A book about
Our women
And she'll be
Amongst those
I pay homage to
Such a lovely
Lady

CHAPTER 4

From the Heart

C H A P T E R   4

From the Heart

These I had great pleasure in writing, for the feelings expressed are actually how I felt toward some women. Thought not too "lucky" in love, the few relationships I've been in for the most part were great. I wouldn't want to relive any of them, but I don't regret that they happened either.

It's just that I consider most of my experiences with black women to have been a blessing. Besides, nobody gets out of life without having gone through something. And as my mother used to say, "If it don't kill you, it'll build you."

I just hope that the impression I left on them wasn't negative.

- A Look into Your Eyes
- That Much Sweeter
- Hello
- The World
- The Time
- On a Walk
- In a House
- Dressed Up
- Your Name
- From Which Garden
- If I Could
- My Prize

A Look into Your Eyes

A look into
Your eyes
Is like
Gazing
Across
The universe
The beauty
Is
Endless,
Captivating

That Much Sweeter

Come to
Me,
Be it
Morning,
Noon,
Or
Night,
For the
Moment
Is always
Special when
You are near,
It makes
What's on
My mind
That much
Sweeter

Hello

To many
Just a simple
Greeting,
But when
Flowing from
Your lips.
An
Exhilarating
Experience,
For what
Accompanies
It,
The world doesn't
Offer enough
Of

The World

To see what
You mean to
Me
You would
Need the
Eyes of God
For only He
Can see
The world

The Time

To see her
Coming is
Such a
Lovely sight,
I now know
Why
I pray,
Someday
She'll be
Mine
Such a warm
Greeting
Regardless of
The time

On a Walk

What are you
On a walk,
The center
Of
Attention
Why so
Many heads
Turn,
Imaginations
Run wild

Dressed Up

What are you
Dressed up,
So beautiful
Words
Can't describe,
When with
Someone
The
Reason his chest
Sticks out,
If alone
What he
Falls to sleep
Thinking about

Your Name

Is there one
Who makes you
Happy,
That while on
Your mind
Causes a smile
To appear on
Your face,
Remind you
Of
The flower
You are,
Great gift
You make,
If not
May I become
Him?
For ever since
I laid eyes
On you,
Every other
Beat of my
Heart.
Calls out
Your name

From Which Garden

From which garden
Were you chosen,
Was it sweet
Like the smell
Of magnolias,
Captivating like
The beauty of
A rose,
When the Creator
Lifted you up,
Did he have to
Reach down into
The valley
For a lily
Or were you
Clinging to your bud
Like a daffodil,

From which garden
Were you chosen
Tell me
I really want
To know,
For I see
The
Carnations,
Daisies,
Violets,
But none of
Them
Are as
Pretty
As you

If I Could

If I could
Be God
For a day,
Here's what I'd do
After finding the
Best
Hairdresser,
Manicurist,
I'd give you
The day off
Then command
The sea to
Give up her dead
And after removing
All of her pollutants,
I'd fill her
With my
Finest fragrances
I'd place
An angel
At each corner
To ward off
All
Planes, ships

And
Spectators
After you were
Dressed for the
Evening,
I'd prepare you a
Gourmet meal
Then rock you to
Sleep
When you arose
The next day,
The sweetest love songs
Ever recorded would
Be playing

My Prize

My prize
Has hair like
Silk
Brown eyes,
Smooth skin,
Luscious lips,
A shape
Like no
Other.
She makes me
Wish
I could live
My life
All over

In a House

What are you
In a house
A reason to
Come home,
Missed,
Before you
Leave

CHAPTER 5

Conclusions

CHAPTER 5

Conclusions

The characteristic I admire the most about our women are their appreciation for life. In saying this, I don't mean in the sense of being born, but thanking God for allowing you to be a participant in his magnificent scheme. Everything and everyone is special and serves a purpose that others can't live without.

Nothing I've experienced has yet to surpass the times me and Mrs. DeziRee Simmons used to spend on her porch—she in her rocking chair, and I on her step. We would talk for hours about God, love, life, politics, history, the future, and even the weather. The value she was back then, and even now, I'll never be able to put into words. Through her, I realized one is definitely a product of how he thinks.

The courage to be thankful can be difficult at times, but as she and so many other black women have shown me, one must be reasonably thankful about something if they wish to get through life. In the midst of my roughest days, she convinced me that I could amount to something. My life, like the river, trees, and others, had a purpose and a need God placed me here to fulfill.

"Stop worrying," she would chastise me, "God knows what he is doing." Most people won't appreciate what you do for them, but the few who do will make you forget all those who didn't.

So here, I compared the many benefits I received from our women to those we receive from nature.

- Black Women Remind Me of the Beach
- Black Women Remind Me of the Bible
- Black Women Remind Me of Books
- Black Women Remind of Forests
- Black Women Remind Me of Gardens
- Black Women Remind That in Time
- Black Women Remind of a Long Walk
- Black Women Remind Me of the Rain
- Black Women Remind Me of the Sunrise
- Black Women Remind Me of Watches
- Talking with a Black Woman

Black Women Remind Me of the Beach

Black women
Remind me
Of the
Beach,
For you can
Go to them
Every day,
And still be
Moved,
Leave,
Looking
Forward
To
Your
Next
Visit

Black Women Remind Me
of the Bible

Black women
Remind me
Of the
Bible,
For in them
Is so much
Strength,
Often when down
I recall
Something one
Taught me
While
Growing up,
And before long
All is well,
Like when
I
Pray and read
Scripture

Black Women Remind Me
of Books

Black women
Remind me
Of
Books
For they
Are quite
An adventure
Uplifting,
Funny,
Exciting,
Full of
Information
Can provide
Great pleasure
When fully
Appreciated

Black Women Remind Me
of Forests

Black women
Remind me
Of
Forests,
The
Beauty
You see
Is only
A spectacle
Of what
Lies within
Full of life

Black Women Remind of Gardens

Black women
Remind me
Of
Gardens,
They don't
Need
Much
Time or space
To
Produce
A
Good harvest

Black Women Remind Me That in Time

Black women
Remind me
That in time,
God answers
All prayers
For their
Ability to
Smile in
The midst
Of
All this
Adversity
Is truly
Amazing

Black Women Remind Me
of a Long Walk

Black women
Remind me
Of
A long walk,
There's
So much joy
In them,
That to
Describe
One
Is impossible

Black Women Remind Me of the Rain

Black women
Remind me
Of
The rain,
For when
They arrive,
Someone
Benefits,
It may not
Be immediately,
But once gone
Someone
Is
Looking
Forward to
Their return

Black Women Remind Me of the Sunrise

Black women
Remind me
Of
The sunrise,
The warmth
I feel
When I see
One coming,
Shall never
Dim

Black Women Remind Me of Watches

Black Women
Remind me of
Watches
It's great to
Have access to
One

Talking with a Black Woman

Talking with
A
Black woman
Is
Like therapy,
Once over
You
Feel
Much better

CHAPTER 6

Around the World

CHAPTER 6

Around the World

Of all the things I discovered through research, none was as rewarding as realizing our women's contributions to the world wasn't a recent phenomenon. Their roles and influence on other cultures are too numerous to list here. I feel I owe just as much thanks to the Queen of Sheba as I do to Zora Neale Hurston and Mary Singleton. How much Cleopatra was admired is a standard I doubt will ever be matched.

The qualities these forbearers possessed, I've witnessed in many black women. The way they balance career, family, and homes to me is truly amazing. The absence of a father, menial jobs, and a disproportionate level of abuse is just as common in other countries as it is in ours. Yet, you don't hear black women griping or witness too many throwing in the towel.

Once while in the mall, I watched this younger sister—she couldn't have been no more than twenty—transport herself, two babies, and her bags out to her

car. I relayed this story 'cause I remember how some brothers were standing around betting she couldn't do it. To make a long story short, she ended up with at least twenty extra dollars, smiled, then remarked, "Never underestimate the power of a sister. Now, hand it over."

- Mothers, Daughters, Sisters
- The Black Woman and the Lioness
- You and the River
- The Sand
- Queen of the Congo
- The Ivory Coast's Sparkle
- Queen of the Nile
- The Treasure of the Islands
- Wherever

Mothers, Daughters, Sisters

The things
I've heard about
Elephants,
How they weep
Over
Their departed
The
Grandmas,
Daughters,
Cousins,
Even
Nieces and Sisters
Work as a unit
So that
The family structure
Remains intact,
Never want for
Anything,
End up
Lost
Divided,
I marvel at this,
For from someone,
Elephants acquired
Such fine example
I wonder was it
From their
Observing
Eve raise hers,
Then decided

This is how
We're going to
Conduct ourselves,
The Elephant's
Wisdom
Habits,
So similar
Are they to
Black women's

The Black Woman and the Lioness

The black woman
And
The Lioness
Have much in
Common,
Not only are
They beautiful,
But the preserver
Of their packs,
Never far from home
And at sunrise
Busy themselves
So
The men and children
Can eat

You and the River

The river
Has been
Abused,
Abandoned,
Taken for
Granted
But yet,
She flows
Undaunted,
Determined
To contribute
Are you
And
The river
Related

The Sand

The sand
Although
Seldom noticed,
Is a mighty
Being,
Has contributed
To mankind
More than
Anyone
God created,
Cleansing,
Correcting,
Protecting,
Providing,
Just like
You

Queen of the Congo

You need not
Adorn
Your skin
With
Gold and gems
To look
Pretty,
Beauty protrudes
From your
Countenance,
Swim daily
Across your face,
Leaps from your
Mouth,
Once looked upon,
Not soon
Forgotten
Queen
Of
The Congo

The Ivory Coast's Sparkle

The Ivory Coast's
Sparkle
Is the
Desire of
All mankind,
She is wise,
Solid as
A mountain,
Swifter than
A river,
Lovely like
A flower,
Breathtakingly
Beautiful
Like
An Autumn
Sunset,
The Ivory Coast's
Sparkle is
A black woman

Queen of the Nile

Queen
Of
The Nile,
Whose hair dangles
Like silk,
Skin softer than
The banks upon
Which you tread,
You are
A beautiful woman,
Spiritually and mentally
With the least
Amount of effort,
You brighten paths,
Illuminate gatherings
Queen
Of
The Nile

The Treasure of the Islands

The treasure
Of
The Islands,
Isn't its
Exotic people,
Places,
Sandy beaches,
Sparkling waters,
Picturesque mountains,
Lush forests,
One can't help
But notice,
The treasure
Of
The Islands,
Is
The one
I love,
Black like
Me,
Beautiful as she's
Made my
Life

Wherever

Wherever
There's
A
Black woman,
God
Ain't too
Far
Away,
Behind

CHAPTER 7

Historically Speaking

CHAPTER 7

Historically Speaking

Although brief, here I try to expound on how black women impact the lives of those immediately around them. On many occasions while talking with others, especially black men, I found it rather startling how they spoke so highly about women besides those in their immediate family. It was from these conversations I ceased wondering, had I loved my mother too much.

Many women probably won't agree with this, but I believe if they would just appreciate the difference between themselves and men, they could have an even greater impact on life. The fact that many of today's women don't enjoy being a woman is one of our greatest tragedies.

- The Black Woman in America
- Freedom, Lord, Freedom
- I'm Sure at Times
- My Babies Gotta Eat
- Dog You Get
- Black Mother to Son
- What Is a Black Sister?
- What Is a Black Niece?
- What Is a Teenage Black Girl?
- What Are Young Black Girls?
- Diamonds in the Rough
- In the Company of Sisters

The Black Woman in America

For years,
The kitchen
And
The bedroom
Were the
Only places
She could receive
Any honor
Despite
An unparalleled quench
For knowledge,
Courage even now
Admired,
Slut,
Cook,
Evil,
Was how society
Referred to this
Matriarch,
Difference in so
Many lives

Now she doesn't
Care,
And our nation
As a whole
Is suffering
Surprised,
Don't be
Just goes to
Show you,
When you shout
Something long enough,
Somebody responds

Freedom, Lord, Freedom

The prayers
Of
Our grandmothers
Guides us even
Now,
The ground is
Soaked with their
Tears,
The herbs
Of
The fields stained
With their blood,
They cried,
Lawd look
After
My seed,
Put a song
In their
Mouths,
Joy in their
Hearts,
They gon need
Freedom
Jesus
Freedom,
Jobs,
Homes,
Each other,
This heah
World is wicked

Father,
I long to
See them
On the
Other side,
Smart,
Happy,
Owned by
No one,
Just like you
Gon make me,
When you
Call me home

I'm Sure at Times

I'm sure
At times,
Bus stops
Would've been
A great place
To be,
For what greater
Reward could
One receive
Than
That of
A black woman
Humming
Her favorite
Hymn,
So grateful
With the little
She had,
It reminded
God
Jesus didn't
Die in vain

My Babies Gotta Eat

Rain
I know you
Must fall,
But today,
You gon
Hafta wait,
I won't be
Long,
All I gotta
Do is dress,
Double-check
To make
Sure everything
Is okay,
Then catch
This bus,
I can't afford
To stay home,
My babies
Gotta
Eat

Dog You Get

Dog you
Get back in
That yard,
I ain't
Botherin' you,
My business
Is much too
Important
To be
Worried bout
Yours,
My bones may
Be Brittle,
But I'll take
This pocketbook
And knock
You out

Black Mother to Son

Many nights
I went to bed
Hungry,
So you could
Eat,
I let the
Elements of nature
Pound against
My skin
So you could
Have clothes
To wear,
Shelter
Over your head,
Your happiness
Is all that
Ever mattered to
Me,
Your life means
More to me
Than my own,
You are the
Apple
Of my eye,
My soul's delight,
I hope and pray
Life
Deals you
A better hand
Than it has

Me,
I'm not ashamed
Of myself
But I'm afraid,
I know
Your struggles
Will be hard
But don't
Give up,
Make me proud,
I want
The world to
Know
You are
My son
And
I love you
Don't ever be
Afraid to
Ask me
Anything,
Cause if
I don't know
The answer,
I'll help you
Find it

What Is a Black Sister?

She is
A reminder
Of
How special
It is
To be
A member
Of our race,
A second
Mother,
Best friend,
Someone
You never
Forget

What Is a Black Niece?

She is a
Reminder
Of
The joy
You've known
And will
Always
Possess,
A flower
You never stop
Nurturing,
Pray
A Great Gardener
Finds
Keeps pruned
So that none
Of
Life's seeds
Ever threaten
Her existence

What Is a Teenage Black Girl?

She is
The essence
Of
Things hoped
For,
The desire
For youth
Once more,
Beautiful
Like a song,
Inspiring
Like a poem,
Thought
Of
Even during
Prayer,
Rejoiced
Over
While away

What Are Young Black Girls?

What are
Young
Black girls,
The
Delight
Of
Someone's
Eyes.
Anticipation
Of
A bright
Future,
Why God
Is
So thanked,
Never forgotten,
Incredibly
Wise,
Amazingly
Gentle

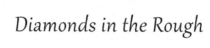

Diamonds in the Rough

If you think
Diamonds
In the rough
Don't exist.
Then you
Should listen
To the
Testimonies
Of
Black women,
And you'd see
How good
It is to
Serve the Lord,
Receive proof
That faith works
Learn
How with
A little money
And
Refusing to
Compromise
Your morals,
You can
Make it,
Put children
Through college,
Steer
Young men in
The right direction

In the Company of Sisters

In the
Company
Of
Sisters
Is a
Great place
To be,
For God
Is there,
You receive proof
He's real,
Get reminded
There's hope
For mankind
Learn to
Grow,
Love,
Forgive,
Their strength
Will astound
You,
Wisdom guide
You,
Touch like
Nothing you'll
Ever feel,
In the
Company
Of
Sisters

Is joy,
No one is
Put down,
Goes hungry,
Get left
Behind,
I know,
I was raised
By black women

CHAPTER 8

Biblically Speaking

CHAPTER 8

Biblically Speaking

History has been rather silent on the fact that many of the Bible's major figures were people of color. The few times it has been acknowledged usually conferred the many negative stereotypes associated with blacks (i.e., Solomon's womanizing, Delilah's treachery, Nimrod's rebellion, and Jonah's cowardice). Uriah's wife, Bathsheba, whom David had murdered, was a black woman. Ruth, the heroine of the book bearing her name and great-grandmother of Israel's most revered king, came from a region wherein its inhabitants were dark-skinned and, as Boaz discovered, were quite attractive.

In no way am I attempting to refute or present any evidence of other black people in the Bible. It's just that the love, courage, and difference, these women showed reminded me of some of the black women who raised me. As with them, I feel their contributions have not only been grossly overlooked

but unappreciated as well. The most important lesson history has shows us many have yet to accept: no race has a monopoly on any characteristics.

- The Balm in Gilead
- Eve Comforts Adam
- Abraham Whispers to Sarah
- Isaac Sees Rebecca Coming
- Jacob's Apology to Rachel
- Joseph Remembers Rachel
- Miriam
- Hannah's Prayer
- What Boaz Thought after Seeing Ruth
- Beautiful Bathsheba
- Solomon Whispers to Shulamite
- Esther Assures Mordecai
- Mary Magdalene Annoints Jesus's Body for Burial
- Solomon Beholds the Queen of Sheba

The Balm in Gilead

Are you
The
Balm in Gilead,
Often
I wonder
For what
Many are expecting
From it,
Reminds me
Of
That I've
Received from
You

Eve Comforts Adam

Sweetheart
Don't
Be down,
The Lord
Has
Given us
Another child,
To
Dwell on
What happened
Isn't fruitful
I miss him to,
The Lord will
Remove
This sorrow
We're
Experiencing
So smile
Okay,
Someday we'll
Know joy
Again
And what
The Lord
Doesn't provide
You with,
I will

Abraham Whispers to Sarah

There's only
One woman for
Me
And her name
Is you,
She is
My thoughts,
My rest,
My labor,
So
Important
That I can't
Describe,
So
Special that
I can't say,
There's only
One love for
Me
And her name
Is you,
I love her
More than myself
Because
Of
You,
Every experience
I have will
Be sweet,
Every moment

I could relive,
You remind me
Of
God,
Wise,
Great
To know,
My
Best friend

Isaac Sees Rebecca Coming

Lord
Let her be
Mine,
For ever since
I
Beheld her,
I've
Been over whelmed
She reminds me
Of
The stories
I've heard about
You,
Good for my
Soul,
A treasure
I'll never let
Go

Jacob's Apology to Rachel

Pardon me my
Love,
But I didn't
Treasure you
Like I should
Have,
I fulfilled my
Desires,
Neglected your
Needs,
And now you're
Gone,
My life is
Empty,
Full of regret
'Cause I can't
Hold you
Anymore

Joseph Remembers Rachel

The beat of
My heart,
Stability of
My mind,
It's as if
You never left
Me
Still I see
You,
Hear your voice,
Everyday the value
Of
What we shared
Increases
And if I could
I'd trade
The many I
Rule over,
All of my
Possessions
For
A moment
With you

Miriam

Much didn't
Need to occur
Before
Miriam was
Thoroughly
Convinced
God would make
A way,
Was worthy of
Praise,
We serve
A great God,
The only
God,
Triumphantly
She proclaimed this,
Many times
Reminding
Moses himself

Hannah's Prayer

Hannah's prayer
Not only comforts
But reminds all that
God is in control
Those who
Believe in Him
Have nothing to
Fear
Much to look
Forward to
Amen

What Boaz Thought after Seeing Ruth

She made
The prettiest blossoms
Seem dull,
Since looking at
Her,
How it would feel
If she was mine
Is all I can
Think about,
Reminding me of
How great God
Is
The opportunity to
Meet her,
I can't let pass
Tomorrow,
I will inquire of
Her
They say God
Answers prayers,
I hope
He's listening to
Mine,

Dear Lord,
I'm in love
The beauty my
Eyes beheld
I want to nourish
Like you do
The heavens
The stars
For I know
The delight your
Works bring
I'll receive from
Her
Amen

Beautiful Bathsheba

Beautiful Bathsheba
Mother of
The wisest man
Who ever lived,
Through whose lions
Came man's
Greatest gift
Beautiful Bathsheba
Whose
Attractiveness,
Appealed to one
So profoundly
He killed to
Have her,
Preserver of humanity
Whose faith
Got the one
God intended to
Rule
Ordained king
Without her sacrifice,
The world
May have already
Ended,
Beautiful Bathsheba
A black woman

Solomon Whispers to Shulamite

Every time
I behold you,
I feel
Rewarded,
Your presence
Reminds me
My living isn't
In vain,
That if I stay
The course I'm on,
I won't have
Anymore problems
If I had
The world to
Give you
Still I'd want to
Give you more,
For what you've
Given me,
Makes you worthy
Of my best,
You've heard this
A thousand times,
But to me it's
Still new,
I love you

Esther Assures Mordecai

I'm with you
That you can
Believe,
I couldn't sleep
At night
Knowing
My fortune
Was at the
Expense of someone
Else,
I'd rather go
Without,
As for my
Intentions,
Don't worry,
In time you'll
See
Nothing has ever
Meant
As much to me
As you,
Your best I've
Always treasured

Mary Magdalene Anoints
Jesus's Body for Burial

Come here baby,
Pardon me
For
Using this new
Oil,
I know it
Could've gone
Towards
Something else,
But
Then again,
I think you
Deserve the best
There,
Don't worry
Everything is gonna
Be alright,
I been praying
For you

Solomon Beholds the Queen of Sheba

Girl
If need be,
I'll make up
Something to
Tell you,
My God she
Makes the best
I've had
Seem second rate,
Whew!
Everything about
You
Baby just drives
Me,
Seems to sing
Your lips,
Your eyes,
And your,
Mm mm mm
I gotta have
Me
Some of that,
Your highness
Hunh,
You say something?

CHAPTER 9

Strictly for Laughs

CHAPTER 9

Strictly for Laughs

Some of this I've
Personally experienced
Some of it I haven't
Which, I won't divulge
I'll leave that for
You to ponder
So if we shall
By chance meet
Don't ask, 'cause I'm not
Gonna tell you
Just enjoy
Here is where I bow out
Repeating what I'll always say
I love you
With your "bad" self

- All The Good Ones
- All That
- Baby Got More Than Back
- The Bomb
- She Caught Me Looking
- Cruising
- Girlfriend
- Her
- Honey Chile
- I'll Be Back
- Miss Thang
- You Go Girl
- Can I Come Over

All the Good Ones

All the good
Ones
Seem to be
Taken,
Too old,
Or mad,
And this leaves
A brother like
Me very sad,
For
When I come
Home,
I prefer to
Be reminded
Of my
Mother, teacher,
And friend,
Not
Arguing
Wondering
Where she's going
When she leaves,
Or
Should I return
While I'm away

All That

All that
And I'll buy
You
The cheeseburger,
French fries,
And drink
The sofa and cable
Too,
If it'll win
Me your heart
The chance
Of
Being seen with
One so breathtaking,
I can show off
Become the topic
Of
The fellas'
Conversation,
(Dam he lucky)
As for
The flowers and gifts,
Trust me
They're on the
Way

Baby Got More Than Back

Baby got more
Than back,
Baby got
My
Heart, mind,
And emotions
Baby also got
Me worried,
For three hours
Have elapsed since
I tossed
Baby my wallet
Then said,
Henh
Go buy you
Something nice,
Now I sit nervous,
About to fall
Apart,
Three of my
Credit cards
Are charged to
The max

The Bomb

Every time
I see her,
Flames of desire
Erupt
Within me,
My mind goes
Blank,
Heart pounds,
Eyes stretch,
I gotta have
This girl,
Lord
What I'd give
For
Smoother lines,
Better threads,
More dough,
Cause
The bomb
Is about to
Drive me
Crazy

She Caught Me Looking

She caught me
Looking
But I don't
Care
Probably mad
So ain't
Gon impede upon
My happiness
Shouldn't have been
So damn fine
Cutting her eyes
So
Next time she's
In the mirror
I'm sure she'll understand
Why she
Caught me looking

Cruising

Cruising in the
Tacoma,
And out of
The corner
Of
My eye
What do I
Happen to see,
A smoking sister,
Once again find
Myself dreaming,
Lord
I wish this
Was a BMW,
Wish I played
For the Jaguars,
Then I could
Go over and
Introduce myself,
Here's something for
Your hair,
Your nails,
A few new dresses,
Flowers,
This my card
Call me girl
And soon

Girl Friend

Girl friend
Is
Something,
Her influence
Widespread,
She causes
Arguments
When speaking,
Listened to
Intently,
Sisters follow
Her advice,
Confide in her,
She in return
Selects
Their
Mates, wardrobes,
Changes their
Minds, hairstyles,
Attitudes,
Girlfriend
A brother's worst
Enemy

Her

I saw her
And immediately concluded,
She could be mine,
That's how I'd like
My wife to look,
Good thing I'm not rich
'Cause I'd be making a
Fool of myself,
God what a woman
So glad I'm black

It's later and I'm
Fortunate enough to see
Her up close,
My heart is melting,
Her
Dimples so soft and cute,
Her
Smile so inviting,
Her
Eyes so alluring,
Her
Warmth unbelievable,
The night we go out,
Stars ya'll better be extra bright,
You too sky and moon
I know she didn't mean
To arouse me,
Just doing her job

We start chatting,
I can hardly breathe
Swear I'm not lusting,

Just beside myself
I'm dreaming I'm rich
We're getting married,
I'm showing her off in
Front of the fellas,
Chest stuck out as they
Drool,
Asking, uhm, uhm
Nathan where you meet her
SHIT?
She has any sisters, enemies, friends
People she useta beat up
DAM?
Figured that short dress
From JCPenney's would do the
Trick
Credit card charged to the max
But I don't care,
Look at my baby,
That's right she's mine

Ain't gon find out if dreams come true
If I don't ask
Praying hard, please Lord,
Dearly as I can
Are you married?
With all her class and I believe
Some concern for me,
I'm engaged she replied
And I almost cried

Honey Chile

Want to know
The latest gossip,
Who hurt who?
Who bout to
Jump something off?
Who after what
Seemed forever
Has finally come to
Their senses,
Ask
Honey chile
She knows,
Stays in the
Middle of something

I'll Be Back

Caramel,
Strawberry,
Chocolate,
Whatever the
Flavor,
I don't care
I'll take you
Anyway,
Long,
Medium,
Short,
You can spend
All my money,
Hurt my feelings,
Just as long as
The last thing
You say is
I'll be back

Miss Thang

Know she cute
Know she fine,
Those tight fitting
Clothes,
Ain't no invitation
But a reminder
Of
What could be yours
If you're a real man
Smooth lines
Don't impress this
Sister,
You must literally
Compliment her,
Reminding
Miss Thang of
The obvious
Won't get you
Nowhere,
Want her?
Who doesn't?
Only the best man
Will be so lucky
Wish he was
Me

You Go Girl

You go girl,
But after
You've been
Please come back,
I try not to
Be jealous,
Act so nervous
When you leave,
Fear somebody will
Take you away,
But it ain't
Easy,
Take a look at
Yourself,
You go girl,
But after you've
Been,
Please come back,
All brothers ain't
Crazy

Can I Come Over

Can I come
Over,
Promise
I won't
Try anything,
I need not be
Near you to
Enjoy the
Many pleasures
You bring,
I've already
Held you,
Kissed you,
Loved you,
And it was
Wonderful

In Closing

Forever

May I call
You
Forever,
For with
All you've
Provided me
With,
It's the only
Name
That seems
Appropriate
For one so
Beautiful

Evaluation Sheet

Use the following questions as a guide if you wish to send me some comments. Thanks a million.

Which chapter was your favorite? Why?

Did you have a favorite poem?

Are there any changes or suggestions you would make (i.e., change in name of volume, chapter, etc.)?

What is your overall evaluation of this work?

What did you like best about it and least about it?

Would you recommend it to friends?

Would you give it as a present to someone?

About the Author

Nathan Brooken, a native of Jacksonville, Florida, began writing songs and poetry while a student at the University of Central Florida in Orlando. *For My Beautiful Black Sister* is his first collection of poems. He is the author of the forthcoming novel, *In Love to Death*. When not writing, Nathan enjoys doing spoken word and is currently at work on a play about this current book of poetry. You can find him on YouTube, Facebook, and Twitter.

CPSIA information can be obtained
at www.ICGtesting.com
Printed in the USA
BVOW09s1049070318
509943BV00001B/29/P